300 PROGRESSIVE SIGHT READING EXERCISES FOR PIANO

Volume 3

The primary goal of this book is to train the ability to read music for the piano without being dependent on finger numbers being provided, such as what one would find in a "Piano-Vocal-Guitar" book — which is the majority of song books for pop, rock, country, etc. (Elton John, The Beatles, and Taylor Swift and so on).

Preview, instructions, video lesson and more:

www.RobertAnthonyPublishing.com

Instructional video links will be posted on the above site as videos are produced.

If this book is helping you, please post a positive review at whichever website you had purchased it from. If you have reqeusts, suggestions or constructive criticism, feel free to use the email link on my website to let me know.

Free pdf downloads of manuscript, keyboard diagrams, and more are available on my website

200 Easy Sight Reading Studies for Piano

Key Signatures: C, G, F, D, Bb, A, Eb, and E Major

Very simple music in a handful of keys to get started

Progressive sight reading in all key signatures up to six sharps and six flats. All pieces have fingerings.

1000 MUSIC READING STUDIES FOR PIANO

Robert Anthony

Table of Contents

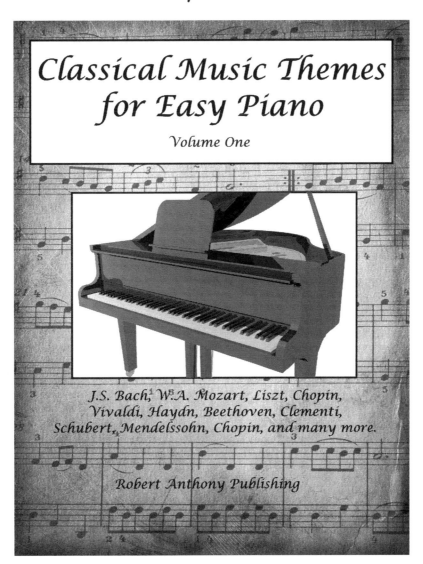

Classical Music Themes for Easy Piano

Volume One

J.S. Bach, W.A. Mozart, Liszt, Chopin, Vivaldi, Haydn, Beethoven, Clementi, Schubert, Mendelssohn, Chopin, and many more.

Robert Anthony Publishing

Foreword:

Volume Three takes a step back in complexity from Volume Two and expands into key signatures up to four sharps and four flats. It is comprised of 300 progressive eight-bar exercises that train reading skills for both hands equally: Half of the pieces emphasize the right hand, the other half emphasize the left. Time signatures include 4/4 (Common Time), 3/4, 2/4, 3/8, Cut Time (2/2), 6/8, and 9/8. Finger numbers have been intentionally excluded from the 300 exercises in order to train the piano player to be able to find their own fingering solutions.

All of the exercises are eight measures long. If one has done any study of formal analysis, they will find that eight measures is a typical 'period' of music and usually contains two, four-bar phrases (also typical in length). For example, many sonatinas, jazz standards, and pop songs use "32 Bar Form" (A A B A), "Binary Form" (A B), and "Ternary Form" (A B A), with each section often being eight bars. Thus, eight measures (one period of music) makes the perfect length for sight-reading studies in my opinion.

How to use this book: Start where the exercises

begin and work across the book — from exercise 1, 5, 9, 13 and so on until you get to a point where the music challenges you and then mark your ending point. The next practice, play exercises 2, 6, 10, 14, and so on... The next: 3, 7, 11, 15 and so on, and finally 4, 8, 12, 16, and so on. If you want to work at your "break point" (the point in the book where you can no longer play musically), work DOWN the page instead of across the pages.

"These books differ from conventional 'methods' in that technical and theoretical instructions have been omitted, in the belief that these are more appropriately left for the teacher to explain to the student." — Bela Bartok, Mikrokosmos.

I whole-heartedly agree with Bartok's sentiment and if music teachers would ask their students what they like least (or hate the most) about typical lessons, it is the method books that win this contest EVERY TIME. I have completely eliminated method books from my own teaching practice and have much happier and more productive students than ever.

Next, the music's composition is a slave to its function: The purpose of the books is to train reading skill, and the exercises keep challenging the range that has been established by previous exercises as well as less-than-convenient intervalic skips. They are composed from a 'music-first' perspective, as opposed to an 'instrument-first' perspective, and are purposely composed to be difficult to memorize.

Some of the music is modal and some uses serial composition technics. Those familiar with the Fundamental Modes and serial composition will likely recognize what they are hearing, but those unfamiliar with these will likely be hearing something that sounds a bit different, or odd, until their ears acclimate to these sounds.

Free pdf downloads at
www.RobertAnthonyPublishing.com

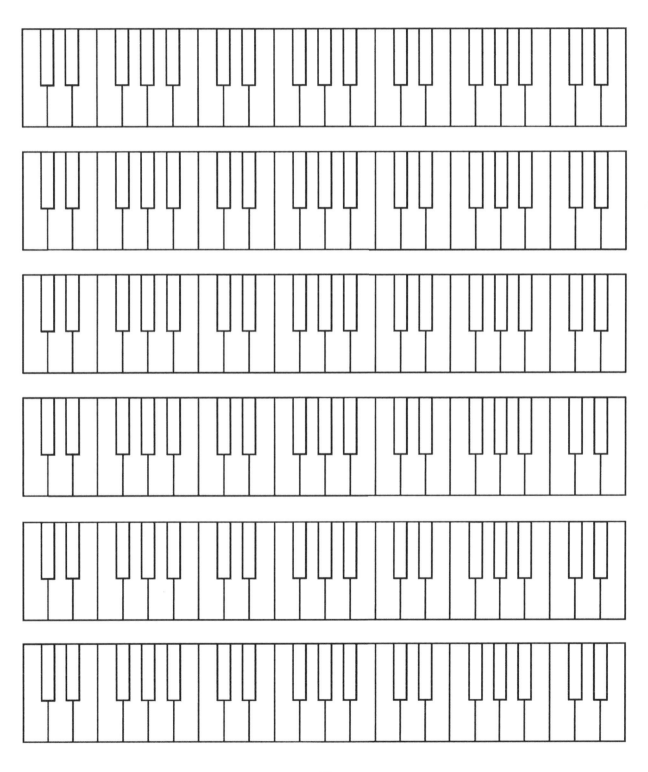

Preview of <u>Children's Piano Method</u>

Two arrangements: left with note names and all fingerings; right with no note names and minimal fingering.

9

Identifying Note Names in Treble Clef

Traditional Approach

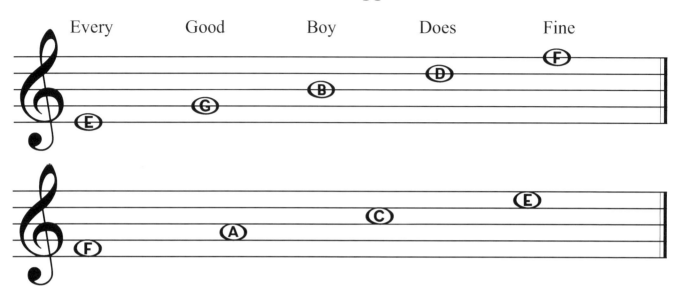

While the traditional approach above is helpful, you will likely find it to be easier to be aware that the musical alphabet (ABCDEFG) simply ascends the lines and spaces of the staff.

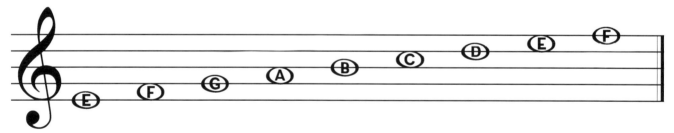

Ledger lines are used to extend the range of the staff as pictured here:

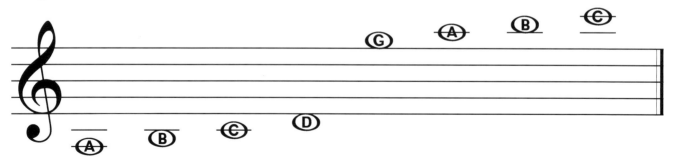

Identifying Note Names in Bass Clef

Traditional Approach

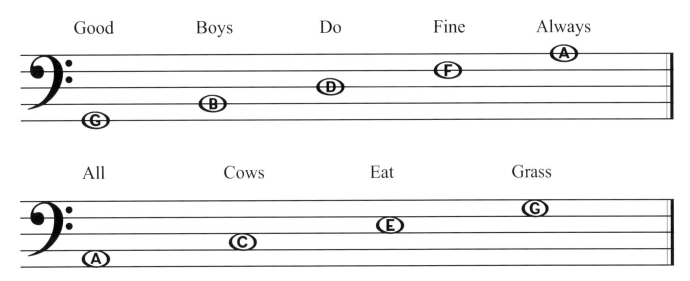

While the traditional approach above is helpful, you will likely find it to be easier to be aware that the musical alphabet (ABCDEFG) simply ascends the lines and spaces of the staff.

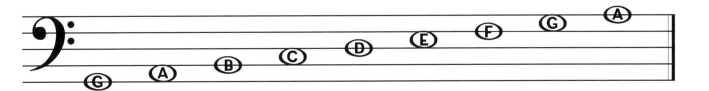

Ledger lines are used to extend the range of the staff as pictured here:

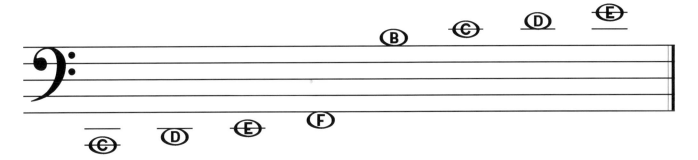

Counting Rhythms in 4/4

Counting Rhythms in 3/4

Counting Rhythms in 6/8

www.RobertAnthonyPublishing.com

Train your common left-hand chord vocabulary while playing the best Christmas Music classics!

Two different levels of difficulty for each song.

Circle of Fifths

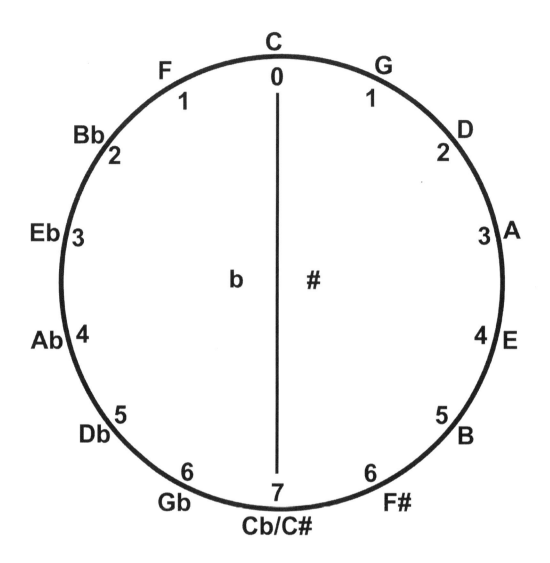

You can use the Circle of Fifths to recognize key signatures by how many sharps (#) or flats (b) are in the key. The key of A Major has three sharps, for example, and the key of Bb has two flats. In the key signatures, sharps always occur in the order: F C G D A E B, while flats always occur in the opposite order: B E A D G C F.

The following sentence will help you to memorize these orders:

Frank's Cat Got Drunk At Elmo's Bar

Major Scales

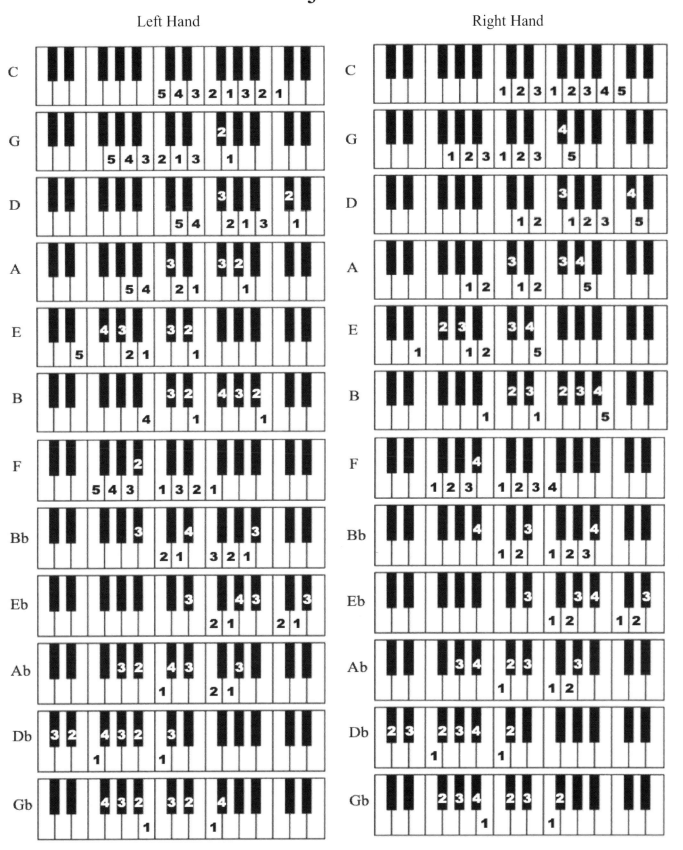

Major Scales, Two Octaves
Sharp Keys

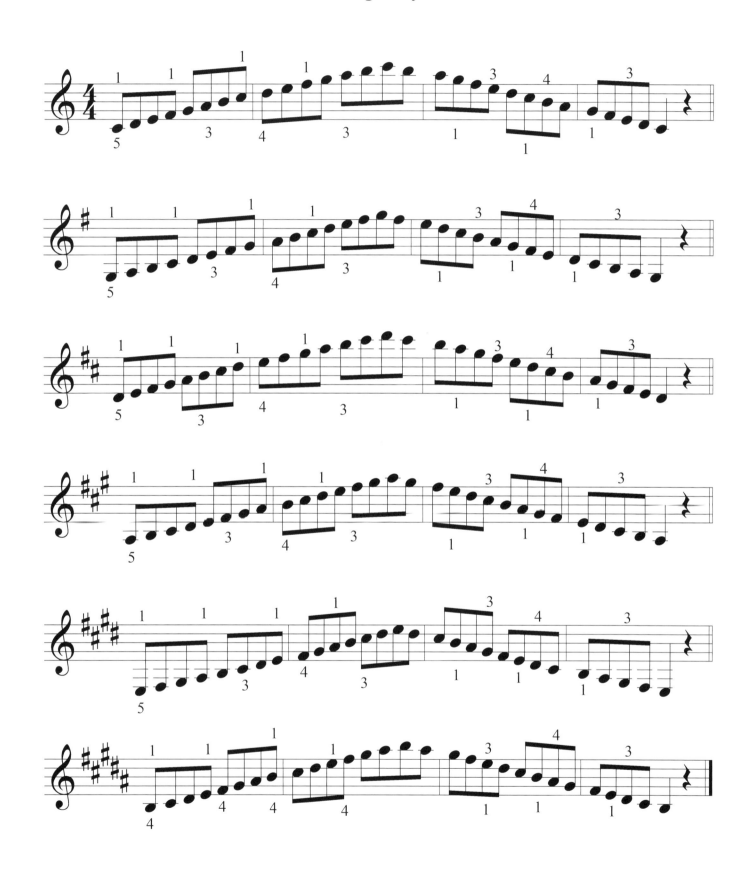

Major Scales, Two Octaves

Flat Keys

1

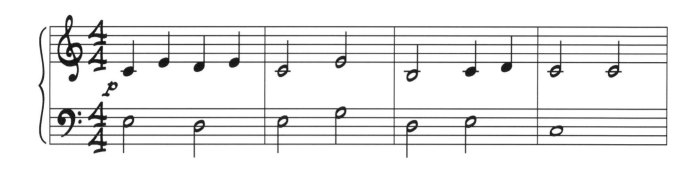

2

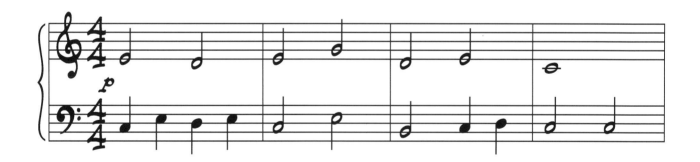

3

4

5

6

9

10

11

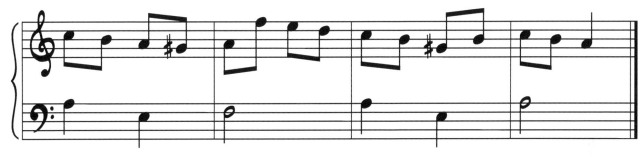

12

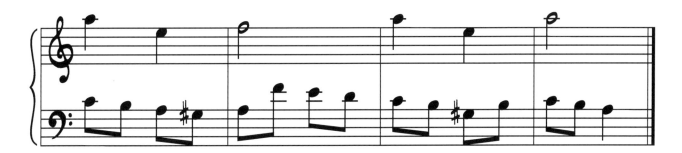

13

14

15

16

17

18

19

20

21

22

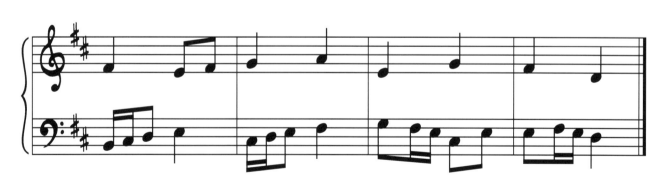

25

26

27

28

29

30

34

31

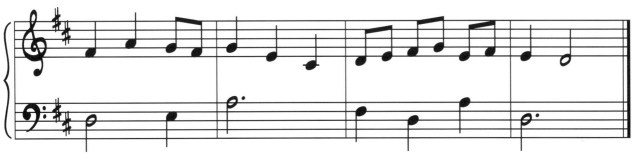

32

40

45

46

47

48

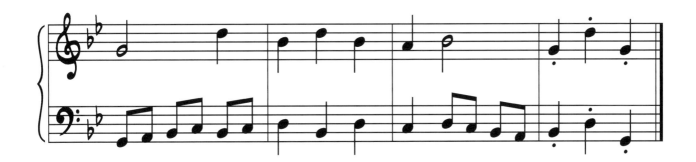

53

54

57

58

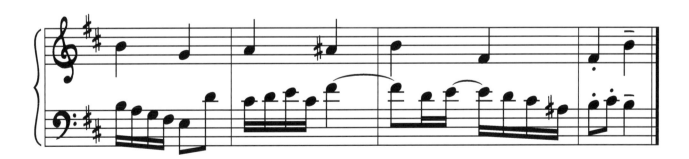

61

62

63

64

65

66

69

70

71

72

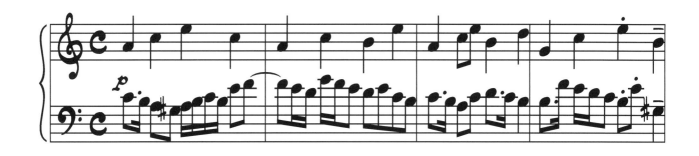

77

78

85

86

62

87

88

89

90

91

92

97

98

109

110

111

112

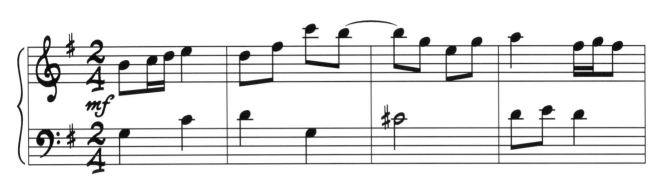

120

123

124

125

126

127

128

139

140

143

144

145

146

147

148

149

150

153

154

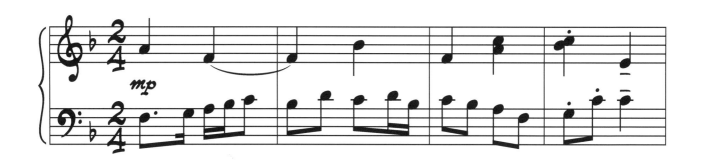

159

160

161

162

163

164

167

168

169

170

175

176

177

178

179

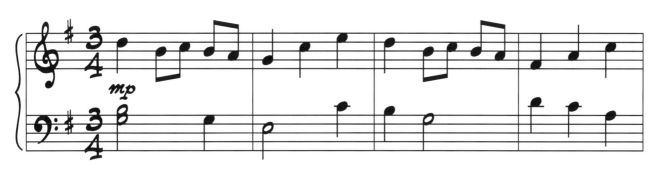

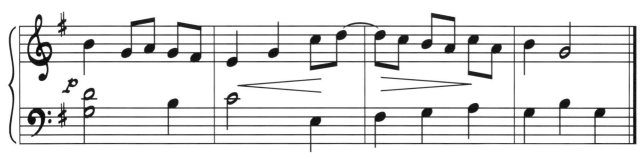

180

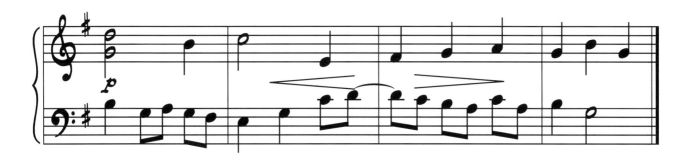

183

184

111

185

186

112

187

188

189

190

191

192

193

194

195

196

197

198

199

200

201

202

203

204

205

206

207

208

213

214

215

216

219

220

221

222

223

224

227

228

229

230

231

232

233

234

235

236

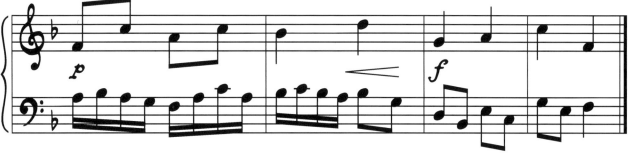

241

242

243

244

245

246

247

248

249

250

251

252

253

254

255

256

262

263

264

265

266

269

270

271

272

273

274

275

276

277

278

279

280

281

282

283

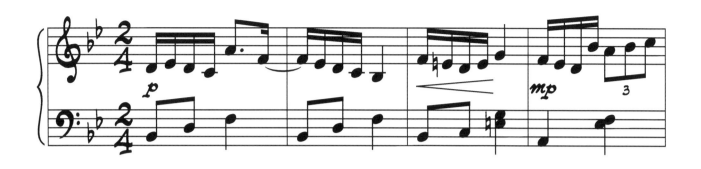

284

285

286

287

288

163

291

292

293

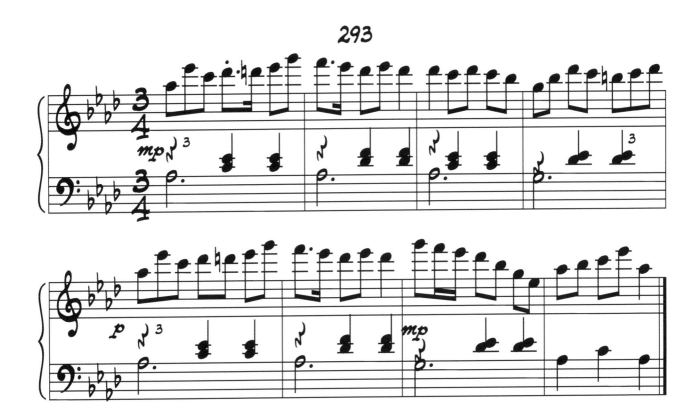

294

296

297

298

299

300

169

Glossary of Musical Terms

Adagio: slowly
Allegretto: fairly fast
Allegro: fast
Andante: moderately slow
Andantino: usually faster than andante
Animato: lively, animated
Cantabile: in a singing style
D.C. al Fine: repeat from the beginning until fine
Dolce: sweetly
Expressivo: expressively
FIne: the end
Grave: very slow, solemnly
Grazioso: gracefully
Lento: very slow
Mesto: sad
Moderato: Medium Tempo
Ritard: slow down
Très Expressif: very expressive
Vivace: lively
Waltz: in three

Dynamic Markings

Pianissimo ~ pp: very softy
Piano ~ p: softly
Mezzo Piano ~ mp: moderately soft
Mezzo Forte ~ mf: moderately loud
Forte ~ f: loud
Fortissimo ~ ff: very loud

**Volumes
1, 2, and 3**

Boldly-printed music. Use these books to train your ability to read music without depending on finger numbers, like what you will find in jazz Real Books, Piano-Vocal-Guitar books of pop, rock, R&B, country, and so on.

15476725R00097